PRAYING FOR YOUR PASTOR'S WIFE

31 DAYS OF GUIDED PRAYER TO STRENGTHEN HER, HER FAMILY, AND HER MINISTRY

CEDAR CREEK MINISTRIES

Copyright © 2026 by Cedar Creek Ministries

All rights reserved.

No part of this publication may be reproduced, stored, or transmitted in any form or by any means, electronic, mechanical, photocopying, recording, or otherwise, without prior written permission from Cedar Creek Ministries, except for brief quotations used in reviews.

Scripture quotations are from the Holy Bible, English Standard Version (ESV®), copyright © 2001 by Crossway, a publishing ministry of Good News Publishers. Used by permission. All rights reserved.

For bulk print licenses or church use, contact:

info@cedarcreekministries.org

Published by Cedar Creek Ministries

Bigfork, Montana

www.cedarcreekministries.org

CONTENTS

Welcome	5
How to Use This Journal	9
Why Pastor's Wives Need Specific Prayer	15
The Biblical Foundation for Praying for Leaders	17
A Note on Confidentiality and Posture	21
A 31-Day Commitment	23
Day 1 Her Worth in Christ	25
Day 2 Confidence in Her Calling	27
Day 3 Freedom from Comparison	29
Day 4 Emotional Strength	31
Day 5 Her Marriage	33
Day 6 Her Friendships	35
Day 7 Physical Health & Rest	37
Day 8 Her Prayer Life	39
Day 9 Protection from Burnout	41
Day 10 Joy in Her Ministry	43
Day 11 Trusting God's Timing	45
Day 12 Overcoming Loneliness	47
Day 13 Freedom from Guilt	49
Day 14 Her Influence on Other Women	51
Day 15 Protection from Spiritual Attacks	53
Day 16 Wisdom in Decision-Making	55
Day 17 Her Heart for Serving	57
Day 18 Peace in the Midst of Conflict	59
Day 19 Her Family Relationships	61
Day 20 Endurance for the Long Journey	63
Day 21 Encouragement in Seasons of Discouragement	65
Day 22 Strengthening Her Faith	67
Day 23 Her Sense of Purpose	69
Day 24 Trusting God with the Unknown	71
Day 25 Finding Joy in the Small Things	73
Day 26 Restoring Her Hope	75
Day 27 Cultivating a Heart of Gratitude	77
Day 28 Protection Over Her Mind	79

Day 29 Boldness to Walk in Her Calling	81
Day 30 Renewed Passion for God's Word	83
Day 31 Blessing Over Her Life and Ministry	85
Take Action Ideas	87
Starting a Prayer Team for Your Church Leaders	97
Recognizing When She May Need Extra Covering	101
A Final Blessing	103
About Cedar Creek Ministries	105
Continue Steadfastly	107

WELCOME

I did not grow up in the church.

I came to faith in my twenties as a young wife and mother, learning what church life even meant as I went. In those early years, I remember the pastor's wives who were kind to me — the ones who made room at their tables, who spoke gently, who saw me when I felt unsure and new.

Over time, something unexpected happened.

One day I looked around and realized that many of my closest, real friendships were with pastor's wives. Not acquaintances. Not "church friends." But women whose lives were woven into mine — women I loved deeply.

And with that love came awareness.

I began to see the quiet pressure they carried. The expectations. The invisible emotional labor. The weight of always being "on." The loneliness that can come even in a room full of people.

It stirred something protective in me. A quiet resolve to stand with these women, not add to their burden.

Through the years of serving with Cedar Creek Ministries, I have had the privilege of walking alongside many pastor's wives. Some have confided deeply. Often, I sensed they felt safe because I did not attend their church, or because I was simply passing through. I was outside the inner circle. There were no expectations to manage.

What I have learned is this:

Pastor's wives do not need more pressure.

They do not need more demands.

They do not need more people who need something from them.

They need prayerful, steady, generous support.

I work hard to be a friend who expects nothing in return. A friend who does not measure access or availability. A friend who understands that seasons change, responsibilities shift, and sometimes even good friendships must ebb and flow.

If a pastor's wife does not have time for a new friendship, it is not personal.

If she pulls back during a heavy season, it is not rejection.

If she seems guarded, it may simply be wisdom.

Trust is built slowly. And it is built best through selfless consistency.

My hope in creating this journal is to help cultivate that kind of heart within the church... a spirit of generosity, hospitality, and quiet strength that does not seek its own.

When we pray faithfully for the women who stand beside our leaders, we become part of the unseen support system that sustains the church itself.

May this month of prayer not only bless her, but shape us into people who carry others well.

With gratitude,
Nickole Perry
& Cedar Creek Ministries Team

HOW TO USE THIS JOURNAL

This journal was created to guide intentional, Scripture-rooted prayer for your pastor's wife.

Not vague well-wishes.

Not surface-level encouragement.

But steady, thoughtful intercession.

You may know her well.

You may barely know her at all.

Either way, prayer does not require proximity, only faithfulness.

A SIMPLE DAILY RHYTHM

Each day includes:

- A focused theme
- A Scripture passage
- A short devotional reflection
- Space to write your prayer

Move slowly. This is not something to rush.

Read the Scripture first.

Let it shape your thinking.

Then pray specifically, using her name.

Writing your prayers helps you pray with clarity and intention.

WHY 31 DAYS?

Because consistency changes culture.

A single kind thought is nice.

Thirty-one days of prayer builds spiritual covering.

As you pray daily, you may notice:

- Greater compassion
- Greater understanding
- A deeper sense of partnership in ministry

Prayer aligns our hearts with God and often with the people we are praying for.

PRAY WITH A FRIEND

Consider inviting one trusted friend to commit to this month with you.

You may choose to:

- Pray separately but check in weekly
- Meet once a week to pray together
- Text one another what you're praying that day
- Share encouragement as you go

There is strength in quiet agreement.

When two women decide to stand in prayer together, the burden feels lighter and faith grows stronger.

IF YOU KNOW HER PERSONALLY

Pray specifically.

- For her marriage
- For her children
- For her friendships
- For her rest
- For the unseen pressures she carries

Let your prayers be detailed and faith-filled.

IF YOU DO NOT KNOW HER WELL

Pray biblically.

Use the Scripture passages as your guide.

Pray over her identity in Christ.

Pray for protection.

Pray for endurance.

Pray for joy.

God knows the details you do not.

WAYS TO USE THIS JOURNAL

This resource may be used:

- Individually during personal devotions
- At the beginning of your women's Bible study as a focused month of prayer
- Handed out church-wide during a prayer initiative
- By an elder or leadership prayer team
- As part of a pastor appreciation season
- During a dedicated Prayer Pledge Drive

Some churches choose to invite the entire congregation into a month of intentional prayer. Others begin with a small group and allow it to grow naturally.

There is no perfect start date only, just start.

A GENTLE REMINDER

This journal is not a place for:

- Criticism
- Assumptions
- Speculation
- Comparison

It is a place for:

- Protection
- Encouragement
- Blessing
- Strengthening

Prayer is one of the most powerful gifts a church can offer its leaders.

AS YOU PRAY

Ask the Lord:

- "How can I support her well?"
- "Is there a small act of encouragement You would have me offer?"
- "Am I cultivating generosity, or expectation?"

Let prayer shape your posture.

This month is not about creating more responsibility for her.

It is about quietly carrying part of the weight.

WHY PASTOR'S WIVES NEED SPECIFIC PRAYER

Pastor's wives are not assistants to ministry.

They are not supporting characters in someone else's calling.

They are women called by God, carrying their own obedience, often under unusual pressure.

While every believer needs prayer, pastor's wives often carry unique burdens:

- Visibility without always having a voice
- Expectations without clear boundaries
- Emotional labor that is unseen
- Spiritual warfare that is intensified
- Loneliness in leadership
- The weight of watching their husbands carry the church

They may be strong.

They may be joyful.

They may be deeply secure in Christ.

And still, they need specific, intentional prayer.

General encouragement is kind.

Specific intercession is strengthening.

When we pray with clarity, we become part of the unseen support system God uses to sustain leaders and their families.

THE BIBLICAL FOUNDATION FOR PRAYING FOR LEADERS

Prayer for leaders is not optional courtesy.

It is biblical responsibility.

Below are several passages that shape our understanding of why and how we pray for those who lead and by extension, the women who stand beside them.

> *"Obey your leaders and submit to them, for they are keeping watch over your souls, as those who will have to give an account... Pray for us, for we are sure that we have a clear conscience, desiring to act honorably in all things."*
>
> — HEBREWS 13:17–18

Reflection:

Spiritual leaders carry eternal responsibility. They watch over souls. They answer to God.

The very next instruction is simple: *Pray for us.*

Prayer is how a congregation participates in leadership without control. It is how we support those who carry accountability we do not see.

When we pray for a pastor's wife, we are strengthening the home of the man who keeps watch over our souls.

> *"Respect those who labor among you and are over you in the Lord... Esteem them very highly in love because of their work."*
>
> — 1 THESSALONIANS 5:12–13

Reflection:

Esteem is more than polite appreciation. It is active honor.

Prayer is one of the highest forms of esteem. It moves beyond compliments and into spiritual covering.

To pray for a pastor's wife is to recognize the labor of ministry and to respond with love, not consumption.

> *"But Moses' hands grew weary... so Aaron and Hur held up his hands... and his hands were steady until the going down of the sun."*
>
> — EXODUS 17:12

Reflection:

Even faithful leaders grow tired.

Aaron and Hur did not criticize Moses for fatigue. They did not demand more strength. They simply stood beside him and held up his arms.

Prayer does this quietly. It steadies what grows weary. It strengthens what feels heavy.

Pastor's wives often help hold up weary arms. Who holds up theirs? Prayer becomes that steady support.

> *"I urge that supplications, prayers, intercessions, and thanksgivings be made for all people, for kings and all who are in high positions..."*
>
> — 1 TIMOTHY 2:1–2

Reflection:

God commands intercession for those in authority.

Church leadership may not look like a throne, but it carries weight and visibility. The spiritual health of a congregation is shaped by those who lead it.

When we pray for those in spiritual authority, including the families who share the cost of that calling, we participate in God's design for peace and stability within His people.

> *"Bear one another's burdens, and so fulfill the law of Christ."*
>
> — GALATIANS 6:2

Reflection:

Burden-bearing is not passive sympathy. It is active participation.

You may not know the details of what a pastor's wife carries. You do not need to.

Prayer allows you to shoulder weight without knowing every circumstance. It fulfills Christ's law through quiet, faithful support.

A NOTE ON CONFIDENTIALITY AND POSTURE

Prayer is powerful. It is also sacred.

This journal is not a space for criticism, speculation, or whispered concern disguised as intercession.

It is not a place to process frustration or compare ministries.

It is a place for protection.

If you are praying in a group, let what is shared remain in confidence. Do not repeat private requests unless you have been given permission.

Guard her story.

Honor her privacy.

Speak life.

Above all, pray with humility. We see only in part. God sees fully.

Let your prayers be shaped by Scripture and love, not assumption.

A 31-DAY COMMITMENT

Prayer grows stronger with intention. If you feel led, mark the start of your 31 days below as a sign of your commitment to steady intercession.

Name: _____

Pastor's wife's name: _____

Start Date: _____

I commit to pray faithfully and to guard my heart in humility and love.

Signature: _____

DAY 1 HER WORTH IN CHRIST

> *"You are my friends if you do what I command you. No longer do I call you servants, for the servant does not know what his master is doing; but I have called you friends, for all that I have heard from my Father I have made known to you."*
>
> — JOHN 15:14–15

Devotional Thought:

A pastor's wife carries a weight that often goes unseen. She is expected to support, uplift, and pour into the lives of those around her, yet she may sometimes feel overlooked. The truth is, before she is a wife, a mother, a leader, or a servant, she is first and foremost a beloved daughter of God. Her worth does not come from her ministry involvement, her husband's role, or the expectations placed upon her. Her worth, like yours, is securely rooted in Christ.

Jesus calls her friend. He knows her name, her heart, and her struggles. He sees her faithfulness, even in the quiet, hidden moments.

When she feels unseen or undervalued, may she find comfort in the truth that the Creator of the universe calls her His own.

As you begin this journey of praying for the pastor's wife, ask God to remind her of her incredible worth. May she feel the deep and abiding love of the Father today, knowing that she is cherished beyond measure.

Prayer:

Heavenly Father, today I lift up _____ to You. Remind her of her immeasurable worth in Your eyes. When she feels unseen or unappreciated, let her rest in the truth that she is Your beloved daughter. Fill her heart with confidence in Your love, and may she find peace in knowing that she is deeply valued—not for what she does, but for who she is in You. Amen.

Take Action:

Write one sentence of affirmation about her identity in Christ and give it to her (text or card).

DAY 2 CONFIDENCE IN HER CALLING

"He who calls you is faithful; he will surely do it."

— 1 THESSALONIANS 5:24

Devotional Thought:

It is easy for a pastor's wife to question whether she is truly called to this role. She may wonder if she is equipped for the unique challenges that come with supporting her husband, balancing ministry responsibilities, and maintaining her own faith journey. The enemy loves to plant seeds of doubt, whispering that she is not enough. But God does not make mistakes. He has called her to this place, and He is faithful to equip her for every good work.

Her calling may not look like her husband's, and that's okay. Some pastor's wives thrive in public ministry, while others serve behind the scenes. Each role is valuable. Her presence, her prayers, and her quiet faithfulness make an eternal impact, even when she doesn't see it.

Today, pray that she will stand firm in the confidence of her calling. May she trust that God has placed her exactly where she needs to be and that He will equip her for every challenge ahead.

Prayer Prompt:

Father, I pray for _____ today. Strengthen her confidence in Your calling on her life. When she feels uncertain, remind her that You have chosen her for a purpose. Remove any doubts that try to take root in her heart. Let her trust in Your faithfulness, knowing that You will give her everything she needs to walk this path with courage. Fill her with peace and assurance that she is exactly where You want her to be. Amen.

Take Action:

Send a 2–3 line encouragement note naming one thing you appreciate about her.

DAY 3 FREEDOM FROM COMPARISON

> *"But let each one test his own work, and then his reason to boast will be in himself alone and not in his neighbor."*
>
> — GALATIANS 6:4

Devotional Thought:

Comparison is a thief of joy. In ministry, it is easy for a pastor's wife to look at others and feel like she falls short. She may see another pastor's wife who is more outgoing, better at organizing events, or seemingly more spiritually mature, and wonder why she isn't more like her. But **God has uniquely gifted her** for the specific place He has called her to.

The church does not need her to be someone else. Her family does not need her to be someone else. **God simply calls her to be faithful with what He has given her.** When she embraces who she is in Christ, she is free to serve with joy, unhindered by the weight of comparison.

Pray today that she will have freedom from the burden of measuring herself against others. May she walk confidently in the path God has set before her, knowing that **she is enough in Christ.**

Prayer:

Lord, I pray for _____ today. Guard her heart against the trap of comparison. Remind her that You have created her with unique gifts and talents that are valuable in Your kingdom. Help her to focus on what You have called her to, rather than looking at what others are doing. Let her find joy in serving You just as she is, knowing that she is fully loved and equipped by You. Amen.

Take Action:

Celebrate, don't compare: compliment your pastor's wife *and* **thank God for how He uniquely made her.**

DAY 4 EMOTIONAL STRENGTH

"God is our refuge and strength, a very present help in trouble."

— PSALM 46:1

Devotional Thought:

Ministry life can take a toll on the emotional well-being of a pastor's wife. She often bears not only her own burdens but also the struggles of her husband, church members, and family. This emotional load can feel overwhelming and isolating at times. She may silently carry the weight of others' grief, conflict, or disappointment while striving to appear strong.

But God is her refuge. He is a safe place where she can lay down her burdens. He is her strength when her own reserves are depleted. She does not need to bear the load alone...He invites her to rest in His presence.

Pray today that she will experience God's sustaining strength in every emotional struggle. Ask that she feels His peace guarding her heart and mind, and that she learns to release her burdens into His capable hands.

Prayer:

Lord, I lift up _____ today. You know the emotional burdens she carries. When the weight feels too heavy, remind her that You are her refuge. Strengthen her heart and renew her spirit. Replace her anxiety with Your peace. Help her to rest in Your presence and trust that You will sustain her through every trial. Amen.

Take Action:

Offer a listening moment: ask, "How are you really doing?" and listen without fixing.

DAY 5 HER MARRIAGE

"And though a man might prevail against one who is alone, two will withstand him—a threefold cord is not quickly broken."

— ECCLESIASTES 4:12

Devotional Thought:

The demands of ministry can put pressure on a marriage. Pastors and their wives often sacrifice personal time together to meet the needs of others. Long hours, late-night phone calls, and emotional exhaustion can leave little room for nurturing their relationship.

A strong, Christ-centered marriage is a powerful testimony. When a pastor's wife and her husband prioritize their relationship and invite God into their union, they become an unbreakable team. Their love and unity can withstand the pressures of ministry when God is their foundation.

Pray today for the pastor's wife and her marriage. Ask that God will strengthen their bond, deepen their love, and protect their time together. Pray that their relationship will be a source of joy and security.

Prayer:

Father, I pray for the marriage of _____ and her husband. Protect their relationship from the pressures of ministry. Help them prioritize time together and nurture their love. May their marriage reflect Your faithfulness and grace. Bind them together with Your love, and let their union be a testimony to those around them. Amen.

Take Action:

Carry a burden: choose one stress you can lighten this week (meal, childcare, errand, ride, cleanup).

DAY 6 HER FRIENDSHIPS

"A friend loves at all times, and a brother is born for adversity."

— PROVERBS 17:17

Devotional Thought:

The life of a pastor's wife can sometimes feel lonely. She may struggle to form deep friendships because of her role in ministry. Some may hold her at a distance, seeing her as different. Others may place unrealistic expectations on her. She may wonder who she can truly confide in.

Yet, God created us for community. He desires for her to have friends who uplift her, speak truth into her life, and walk alongside her. She needs safe spaces to be vulnerable, to laugh, and to be refreshed.

Pray today that God will bring godly friendships into her life, people who will encourage her, pray with her, and remind her she is not alone. May her heart be open to the relationships God is orchestrating for her.

Prayer Prompt:

Father, I pray for _____. Surround her with godly friends who uplift and encourage her. Let her find safe, trustworthy companions who will walk with her through both joys and trials. Help her heart to be open to the friendships You provide. Bless her with rich, life-giving relationships. Amen.

Take Action:

Protect their marriage time: offer to help so they can have one uninterrupted hour together.

DAY 7 PHYSICAL HEALTH & REST

"He makes me lie down in green pastures. He leads me beside still waters. He restores my soul."

— *PSALM 23:2–3A*

Devotional Thought:

The demands of ministry can lead a pastor's wife to neglect her physical health and rest. She may be constantly on the go, serving others while pushing her own needs aside. Over time, this can lead to exhaustion and burnout.

God cares about her physical well-being. He designed our bodies to need rest and renewal. He invites her to come to Him, to lie down in green pastures, and to be refreshed by His presence.

Pray today that she will prioritize her health. Ask that God helps her find rhythms of rest and refreshment. May she care for her body as a temple of the Holy Spirit, faithfully pouring out in service to others while trusting God for her own renewal.

Prayer Prompt:

Lord, I lift up _____. Help her to prioritize her physical health and find rest. Guard her against burnout. Refresh her body and soul. Lead her beside quiet waters, and restore her strength. Teach her to embrace the rest You provide. Amen.

Take Action:

Be a safe friend: invite her for coffee/walk with zero agenda and no church talk required.

DAY 8 HER PRAYER LIFE

"The Lord is near to all who call on him, to all who call on him in truth."

— PSALM 145:18

Devotional Thought:

A pastor's wife often prays for others; her husband, her children, the congregation, but her personal prayer life can sometimes become neglected. She may give so much that she forgets to come to God for herself.

God longs for her to come to Him. He invites her to bring her burdens, fears, and hopes into His presence. Her strength is renewed when she abides in prayer, finding intimacy with her Heavenly Father.

Pray today that her prayer life will be vibrant and consistent. Ask God to draw her into deeper communion with Him, that she will find rest, wisdom, and peace in His presence.

Prayer:

Father, I pray for _____. Renew her passion for prayer. Draw her heart closer to You. Let her find comfort and strength as she pours out her soul before You. May she know You are near, listening to every word. Bless her time with You. Amen.

Take Action:

Encourage rest: gift her an hour back (babysitting, drop-off help, or a quiet house window).

DAY 9 PROTECTION FROM BURNOUT

"Come to me, all who labor and are heavy laden, and I will give you rest."

— MATTHEW 11:28

Devotional Thought:

Burnout is a silent struggle for many pastor's wives. The constant demands of ministry can leave her feeling emotionally, physically, and spiritually drained. She may pour into others until she has nothing left for herself.

But Jesus offers rest. He invites her to come to Him and to lay her burdens at His feet. True rest is found in His presence, where her soul can be renewed. She is not meant to carry the weight of ministry alone; God desires to strengthen and sustain her.

Pray today that she will recognize the warning signs of burnout and seek God's rest. Ask that she learns to manage life well and trust God to fill the gaps. May she find refreshment in the Lord, knowing He is her strength.

Prayer:

Lord, I lift up _____. Guard her heart and mind against burnout. When she feels overwhelmed, lead her to Your rest. Teach her to set boundaries and to trust that You are in control. Refresh her spirit and remind her that her worth is not measured by what she accomplishes but by Your love. Amen.

Take Action:

Pray specifically: ask one question about what she needs prayer for, then pray that same day.

DAY 10 JOY IN HER MINISTRY

"Do not be grieved, for the joy of the Lord is your strength."

— NEHEMIAH 8:10

Devotional Thought:

Ministry can sometimes feel more like a burden than a blessing. A pastor's wife may grow weary from criticism, unmet expectations, or simply the weight of responsibility. In those moments, her joy can fade.

But God's joy is her strength. When she shifts her focus from the pressures of ministry to the faithfulness of God, her spirit can be renewed. Joy is not rooted in circumstances. Joy is found in the presence of the Lord.

Pray today that her heart will be filled with joy. Ask that she will see the fruit of her labor and find delight in serving. May her ministry be marked by laughter, gratitude, and the unshakable joy that comes from knowing God.

Prayer:

Lord, I pray for _____. Fill her heart with joy today. Let her see the beauty in the work You've called her to. When ministry feels heavy, remind her of the privilege it is to serve You. Let Your joy be her strength, carrying her through every season. Amen.

Take Action:

Support her priorities: honor one healthy "no" she needs to say this month.

DAY 11 TRUSTING GOD'S TIMING

"For everything there is a season, and a time for every matter under heaven:"

— ECCLESIASTES 3:1

Devotional Thought:

Ministry often involves waiting...waiting for growth, for breakthroughs, for healing, or simply for clarity. A pastor's wife may grow weary in the waiting, wondering when God will move in her situation or answer her prayers.

Yet, God's timing is perfect. He is never late. He sees the bigger picture, weaving together every detail for His glory and her good. Waiting is not wasted when it draws her closer to Him.

Pray today that she will trust God's perfect timing. Ask that she finds peace in knowing He is at work, even when she cannot see it. May she rest in His promises, believing that His plans are always best.

Prayer:

Father, I lift up _____. Help her to trust Your timing in every area of her life and ministry. When she grows impatient, remind her that You are always working behind the scenes. Fill her heart with peace and patience as she waits on You. Let her find joy in this season, knowing that You are faithful. Amen.

Take Action:

Bring joy: send something that makes her laugh (a kind meme, a memory, a "you're loved" voice text).

DAY 12 OVERCOMING LONELINESS

"God settles the solitary in a home; he leads out the prisoners to prosperity, but the rebellious dwell in a parched land."

— PSALM 68:6

Devotional Thought:

The role of a pastor's wife can be isolating. She may struggle to form deep connections, fearing judgment or misunderstanding. She may feel like no one truly understands the unique pressures she faces.

But God sees her loneliness. He is her constant companion, drawing near to her in every season. He also provides community, sometimes in unexpected ways. He places the lonely in families, surrounding her with His love through others.

Pray today that she will experience God's presence in her loneliness. Ask that He brings people into her life who offer genuine friendship and support. May she know she is never truly alone.

Prayer:

Lord, I pray for _____. When she feels isolated, remind her that You are always with her. Surround her with loving, understanding friends. Help her to find community where she can be herself. Fill the empty spaces in her heart with Your presence and peace. Amen.

Take Action:

In a waiting season: share one promise Scripture has used to steady you…no lecture, just hope.

DAY 13 FREEDOM FROM GUILT

"There is therefore now no condemnation for those who are in Christ Jesus."

— ROMANS 8:1

Devotional Thought:

A pastor's wife often feels the pressure to meet every need and fill every gap. When she falls short, or simply feels like she does, guilt can creep in. She may believe she is failing her husband, her children, her church, or even God.

But guilt without sin is not from God. His grace is sufficient. In Christ, she is forgiven and free. God calls her to rest in His grace, knowing that her worth is not tied to her performance.

Pray today that she will be released from the burden of unbiblical guilt. Ask that she fully embraces the freedom and grace that Christ offers. May she walk in confidence, knowing that she is loved, accepted, and forgiven.

Prayer:

Lord, I lift up _____. Break the chains of guilt in her life. Remind her that there is no condemnation for those in Christ. Let her rest in Your grace and experience freedom from self-criticism. Fill her with peace, knowing that You are pleased with her. Amen.

Take Action:

Fight isolation: introduce her to one potential friend or invite her into a small, safe gathering.

DAY 14 HER INFLUENCE ON OTHER WOMEN

"She opens her mouth with wisdom, and the teaching of kindness is on her tongue."

— PROVERBS 31:26

Devotional Thought:

Whether she realizes it or not, a pastor's wife is a role model to many women. Her words, actions, and faith are observed by those around her. This influence can feel like a burden, but it is also a beautiful opportunity.

God has positioned her to encourage, uplift, and guide other women. Her authenticity, vulnerability, and wisdom can inspire others to grow in their faith.

Pray today that she will recognize her influence and use it to bless others. Ask God to give her wisdom and grace as she interacts with the women in her church and community.

Prayer:

Father, I pray for _____. Help her see the impact she has on other women. Give her wisdom and kindness in her words. Let her be a source of encouragement and strength. Use her life as a testimony of Your goodness. Amen.

Take Action:

Replace guilt with grace: remind her (briefly) that God is not measuring her by output

DAY 15 PROTECTION FROM SPIRITUAL ATTACKS

"Put on the whole armor of God, that you may be able to stand against the schemes of the devil."

— EPHESIANS 6:11

Devotional Thought:

Those in ministry are often targets of spiritual attacks. The enemy seeks to discourage, divide, and distract those who are building God's kingdom. A pastor's wife is not exempt. She may face doubts, fears, or conflicts that feel overwhelming.

But God equips her for battle. He provides spiritual armor; truth, righteousness, peace, faith, salvation, and His Word. She is not defenseless. With God's strength, she can stand firm.

Pray today for her spiritual protection. Ask that God shields her from the enemy's attacks and strengthens her faith. May she put on the full armor of God each day, standing secure in His power.

Prayer:

Lord, I pray for _____. Protect her from the schemes of the enemy. Guard her heart and mind with Your truth. Strengthen her faith, and remind her that she is victorious through You. Clothe her in Your armor so she can stand firm. Amen.

Take Action:

Speak life about her influence: tell her one specific way she encourages other women.

DAY 16 WISDOM IN DECISION-MAKING

"If any of you lacks wisdom, let him ask God, who gives generously to all without reproach, and it will be given him."

— JAMES 1:5

Devotional Thought:

Pastor's wives often face decisions that affect both their families and their church communities. From navigating personal choices to supporting ministry direction, the weight of these decisions can feel heavy. She may worry about making the wrong choice or struggle to discern God's will.

But God promises to give wisdom to those who ask. He invites her to seek Him in every decision, and He will guide her steps. His wisdom is perfect, and He delights in leading His children.

Pray today that she will seek God's wisdom in every decision she faces. Ask that she will hear His voice clearly and trust His guidance. May she experience peace, knowing that God is directing her steps.

Prayer:

Lord, I lift up _____. Give her wisdom in every decision she makes. When she feels uncertain, remind her to seek You. Speak clearly to her heart, and give her confidence in Your leading. Let her rest in the assurance that You are guiding her steps. Amen.

Take Action:

Cover her spiritually: pray Ephesians 6 over her by name today.

DAY 17 HER HEART FOR SERVING

"Rendering service with a good will as to the Lord and not to man."

— EPHESIANS 6:7

Devotional Thought:

The heart of a pastor's wife is often one of service, whether hosting gatherings, leading women's ministries, or simply offering a listening ear. While this servant's heart is a beautiful gift, it can also lead to exhaustion or feelings of being taken for granted.

God sees her service. He values every unseen act of kindness and every quiet sacrifice. Her work is not in vain when done for Him. Her service is an offering of love to the Lord, and He will reward her faithfulness.

Pray today that her heart for serving will be strengthened. Ask that God renews her joy in service and reassures her that He sees every effort. May she be reminded that she is ultimately serving her loving Savior.

Prayer:

Father, I pray for _____. Strengthen her heart for serving. When she feels weary, remind her that her work is for You. Renew her joy in serving others. Help her see the eternal value in all that she does, and let her find rest in Your presence. Amen.

Take Action:

Offer wise help: ask, "Is there a decision coming up I can pray about with you?"

DAY 18 PEACE IN THE MIDST OF CONFLICT

"Blessed are the peacemakers, for they shall be called sons of God."

— MATTHEW 5:9

Devotional Thought:

Conflict is an inevitable part of ministry. Whether within the church, among staff, or even within her own home, a pastor's wife may often find herself in the middle of tension. This can weigh heavily on her heart as she seeks to maintain unity and peace.

God calls her to be a peacemaker, not by her strength alone, but through the power of His Spirit. He promises to give her wisdom and grace as she navigates difficult situations. True peace is found in Him, even when circumstances are challenging.

Pray today that she will be a vessel of God's peace. Ask that He gives her patience, discernment, and wisdom to handle conflicts with grace. May she rest in the truth that God is her ultimate source of peace.

Prayer:

Father, I lift up _____. When conflict arises, let her heart be guided by Your peace. Give her wisdom to navigate difficult conversations. Help her be a peacemaker, reflecting Your love and grace in every situation. Strengthen her when tensions are high, and let Your presence bring calm to her soul. Amen.

Take Action:

Appreciate her service: name one unseen thing she does and say thank you for it.

DAY 19 HER FAMILY RELATIONSHIPS

"And they said, 'Believe in the Lord Jesus, and you will be saved, you and your household.'"

— ACTS 16:31

Devotional Thought:

Balancing family and ministry can be one of the greatest challenges a pastor's wife faces. She may feel pulled in different directions, trying to meet the needs of her children, support her husband, and care for the church.

God cares deeply about her family. He desires for their home to be a place of love, faith, and unity. He is the one who holds her family together and will work in their hearts as she entrusts them to Him.

Pray today for her family relationships. Ask that God strengthens her bond with her husband and children. Pray that their home will be filled with love, laughter, and faith. May she trust God to work in the hearts of each family member.

Prayer:

Lord, I pray for _____ and her family. Strengthen their relationships. Let their home be a place of peace and joy. Help her find balance between ministry and family. Protect their bond from the pressures of church life, and draw them closer to You and each other. Amen.

Take Action:

Be a peacemaker: refuse gossip/criticism...stop it kindly and redirect.

DAY 20 ENDURANCE FOR THE LONG JOURNEY

"And let us not grow weary of doing good, for in due season we will reap, if we do not give up."

— GALATIANS 6:9

Devotional Thought:

Ministry is a marathon, not a sprint. There are seasons of excitement and growth, but there are also seasons of hardship and discouragement. A pastor's wife may sometimes feel like giving up when the road feels long and the fruit seems scarce.

God calls her to endure, reminding her that the harvest will come in His perfect time. He is her source of strength when she is weary. He promises that her faithfulness will bear fruit, even when she cannot see it yet.

Pray today for her endurance. Ask that God renews her strength and fills her heart with hope. May she be reminded that her labor is not in vain and that God is working through every season.

Prayer:

Lord, I lift up _____. When she feels weary, renew her strength. Remind her that her work is not in vain. Fill her with hope and endurance for the journey ahead. Help her to trust that the harvest is coming in Your perfect time. Amen.

Take Action:

Bless her family: do one tangible kindness for their household this week.

DAY 21 ENCOURAGEMENT IN SEASONS OF DISCOURAGEMENT

"The Lord is near to the brokenhearted and saves the crushed in spirit."

— PSALM 34:18 (ESV)

Devotional Thought:

There will be days when the pastor's wife feels deeply discouraged. Ministry can bring criticism, rejection, or seasons of fruitlessness that weigh heavily on her heart. She may question her effectiveness or even wonder if she is making a difference at all.

But God draws near to the brokenhearted. He sees every tear and hears every prayer. He is the lifter of her head, reminding her that her labor is not in vain. Even when she cannot see the results, He is at work.

Pray today that God will encourage her spirit. Ask that she feels His presence especially near when she is discouraged. May she find strength in His promises and hope in knowing He is always working.

Prayer:

Father, I lift up _____. On the hard days, remind her that You are close. Speak encouragement to her heart. Show her glimpses of the fruit of her labor. Let her find rest and hope in Your unfailing love. Amen.

Take Action:

Strengthen endurance: leave a note that says, "Your faithfulness matters. Keep going."

DAY 22 STRENGTHENING HER FAITH

"Therefore, as you received Christ Jesus the Lord, so walk in him, rooted and built up in him and established in the faith, just as you were taught, abounding in thanksgiving."

— COLOSSIANS 2:6–7 (ESV)

Devotional Thought:

A pastor's wife is often pouring into others, but she needs to be filled too. Her faith journey is personal, beyond supporting her husband or leading in the church, she needs to remain rooted in Christ for her own spiritual growth.

God desires to strengthen her faith day by day. He invites her to abide in Him, to dig deep into His Word, and to trust Him more fully. When her roots go deep, she can withstand the storms of life and continue to bear fruit.

Pray today that her faith will be strengthened. Ask God to give her a hunger for His Word and a desire to grow closer to Him. May she stand firm in faith, knowing that He is her foundation.

Prayer:

Lord, I pray for _____. Strengthen her faith in You. Draw her closer each day. Let her roots grow deep into Your Word. When challenges arise, may she stand firm, trusting in Your promises. Fill her heart with the joy of knowing You. Amen.

Take Action:

Encourage on hard days: send a "no response needed" text: "Praying today. You're not alone."

DAY 23 HER SENSE OF PURPOSE

"For we are his workmanship, created in Christ Jesus for good works, which God prepared beforehand, that we should walk in them."

— EPHESIANS 2:10 (ESV)

Devotional Thought:

It is not uncommon for a pastor's wife to wrestle with her sense of purpose. She may wonder if she is doing enough or if her contributions are truly valuable. She may feel overshadowed by her husband's visible role.

But God has uniquely crafted her for a purpose. She is His masterpiece, designed with gifts and strengths that contribute to His kingdom. Her work, seen or unseen, matters deeply to God.

Pray today that she will embrace her God-given purpose. Ask that He affirms her calling and reveals how her unique role is making an impact. May she walk in confidence, knowing that she is fulfilling His plan for her life.

Prayer:

Father, I pray for _____. Remind her that she is Your masterpiece. Affirm her purpose and reveal the ways You are using her. Let her see the beauty in her unique role. Give her confidence to walk in the work You have prepared for her. Amen.

Take Action:

Fuel her faith: share one worship song, sermon, or passage that refreshed you. Keep it simple.

DAY 24 TRUSTING GOD WITH THE UNKNOWN

> *"Trust in the Lord with all your heart, and do not lean on your own understanding. In all your ways acknowledge him, and he will make straight your paths."*
>
> — PROVERBS 3:5–6 (ESV)

Devotional Thought:

Uncertainty is a reality in ministry life. Plans can change, finances can fluctuate, and the future can feel unclear. A pastor's wife may feel the pressure to hold everything together, even when she has no control over the outcome.

God calls her to trust Him fully. He holds her future in His hands and is guiding every step. She doesn't need to have all the answers because He does. Her role is to submit her fears and plans to Him and rest in His perfect wisdom.

Pray today that she will trust God with the unknown. Ask that He quiets her anxieties and fills her with faith. May she lean on His understanding and find peace knowing He is directing her path.

Prayer:

Father, I pray for _____. When the future feels uncertain, help her to trust You completely. Calm her fears and remind her that You are in control. Guide her steps and give her confidence that Your plans are good. Amen.

Take Action:

Avoid "pastor-wife pressure": ask what support looks like for *her*, not what you assume she should do.

DAY 25 FINDING JOY IN THE SMALL THINGS

"This is the day that the Lord has made; let us rejoice and be glad in it."

— PSALM 118:24 (ESV)

Devotional Thought:

Ministry can often feel like a series of big events and major responsibilities, but much of life is lived in the small, ordinary moments. A pastor's wife may feel like her efforts are only significant when they are seen or celebrated, yet God delights in the simple, everyday faithfulness.

The small things, sharing a kind word, preparing a meal or offering a listening ear are acts of love that reflect God's heart. Joy is found not just in big accomplishments but in noticing His goodness in the quiet, simple moments.

Pray today that she will find joy in the small things. Ask that God opens her eyes to see His goodness in the ordinary. May she experience deep contentment, knowing that every act of love, no matter how small, is valuable in His eyes.

Prayer:

Lord, I pray for _____. Help her to find joy in the little things today. Open her eyes to see Your goodness all around her. Remind her that every small act of faithfulness matters to You. Fill her heart with contentment and delight in each day. Amen.

Take Action:

Confirm her purpose: tell her one strength you see that blesses the church/community.

DAY 26 RESTORING HER HOPE

> *"May the God of hope fill you with all joy and peace in believing, so that by the power of the Holy Spirit you may abound in hope."*
>
> — ROMANS 15:13 (ESV)

Devotional Thought:

Seasons of ministry can sometimes leave a pastor's wife feeling disillusioned or weary. Disappointments, unmet expectations, or prolonged struggles can chip away at her hope. She may wonder if things will ever change or if the burdens will ever lift.

But our God is a God of hope. He offers more than fleeting optimism; He gives a hope that is rooted in His character and promises. Through the power of the Holy Spirit, He can renew her hope, even in the hardest seasons.

Pray today that God will restore her hope. Ask that He revives her spirit and fills her with His joy and peace. May she look to the future with confidence, knowing that God is working all things for good.

Prayer:

God of hope, I lift up _____ to You today. You know the burdens she carries and the moments when her hope has grown dim. I ask that You breathe new life into her heart. Fill her with Your joy and peace as she trusts You. Let her hope overflow—not because circumstances have changed, but because she knows You are faithful. Strengthen her to believe that You are working even now. In Jesus' name, Amen.

Take Action:

Help with uncertainty: offer one practical assist (meal train, ride, schedule help) during unknowns.

DAY 27 CULTIVATING A HEART OF GRATITUDE

"Give thanks in all circumstances; for this is the will of God in Christ Jesus for you."

— 1 THESSALONIANS 5:18 (ESV)

Devotional Thought:

Gratitude is a powerful weapon against discouragement and bitterness. A pastor's wife may face challenges that tempt her to focus on what is lacking or what is difficult. Ministry can expose her to criticism, disappointment, or loneliness. Yet, in the midst of it all, God invites her to give thanks.

Gratitude shifts her perspective. It reminds her of God's faithfulness in the past and opens her eyes to His goodness in the present. When she chooses gratitude, she invites joy and peace into her heart.

Pray today that she will cultivate a heart of gratitude. Ask that God helps her see His blessings even in hard seasons. May thanksgiving become her natural response, bringing light and joy into every area of her life.

Prayer:

Gracious Father, I come before You on behalf of _____. I thank You for the ways You have sustained her and provided for her. When challenges arise, guard her heart against bitterness or despair. Instead, plant within her a spirit of gratitude. Help her see Your hand in both the big and small moments. Let thankfulness fill her lips and lift her spirit. May she reflect Your goodness in all she does. Amen.

Take Action:

Help with uncertainty: offer one practical assist (meal train, ride, schedule help) during unknowns.

DAY 28 PROTECTION OVER HER MIND

"You keep him in perfect peace whose mind is stayed on you, because he trusts in you."

— ISAIAH 26:3 (ESV)

Devotional Thought:

The mind is often the battleground where spiritual warfare is fiercest. A pastor's wife may struggle with anxious thoughts, self-doubt, or lies from the enemy. She may battle feelings of inadequacy, fear, or discouragement that threaten to overwhelm her.

God desires for her to walk in perfect peace. He offers peace that guards her mind and heart when she fixes her thoughts on Him. His truth can break every lie, and His presence can calm every storm in her mind.

Pray today for protection over her mind. Ask that God fills her thoughts with His truth and silences every voice of fear or doubt. May her mind be guarded by His perfect peace as she trusts in Him.

Prayer:

Lord, I lift up _____ and ask for Your protection over her mind. When anxious thoughts creep in, replace them with Your truth. Silence the lies of the enemy and speak words of life and peace into her heart. Strengthen her to take every thought captive and make it obedient to Christ. Let Your perfect peace guard her heart and mind. May she rest in the assurance that You are her refuge and strength. Amen.

Take Action:

Restore hope: write one sentence about a time you saw God be faithful in the long haul.

DAY 29 BOLDNESS TO WALK IN HER CALLING

"The wicked flee when no one pursues, but the righteous are bold as a lion."

— PROVERBS 28:1 (ESV)

Devotional Thought:

A pastor's wife may sometimes shrink back from the calling God has placed on her life. Fear of criticism, self-doubt, or the pressure to meet others' expectations can cause her to hold back. Yet, God calls her to walk boldly in the purpose He has designed for her.

Boldness does not mean being loud or forceful. It is a quiet confidence in God's strength. It is stepping forward in faith, trusting that He will equip her for every task.

Pray today that she will embrace boldness in her calling. Ask that God will remove any fear and fill her with courage.

Prayer:

Father, I lift up _____ before You today. You have called her, and You will equip her. When fear whispers to her heart, silence it with Your truth. Fill her with boldness—boldness that comes from knowing You are with her. Let her walk confidently in her purpose. Strengthen her when she feels weak. Open doors for her to serve and lead in ways that glorify You. Amen.

Take Action:

Model gratitude: thank her publicly (appropriately) or privately. Be brief, specific and sincere.

DAY 30 RENEWED PASSION FOR GOD'S WORD

"Your word is a lamp to my feet and a light to my path."

— PSALM 119:105 (ESV)

Devotional Thought:

In the busyness of ministry and life, it can be easy for a pastor's wife to drift from the richness of God's Word. Her time in Scripture may become sporadic or feel like another task on her to-do list. Yet, God's Word is her source of life, strength, and guidance.

Pray today that God will renew her passion for His Word. Ask that He ignites a hunger within her to seek Him daily.

Prayer:

Lord, I pray for _____. Stir within her a deep hunger for Your Word. When life feels overwhelming, draw her back to the truth of Scripture. Let Your Word be her anchor, her comfort, and her guide. Fill her heart with joy in time spent with You. Amen.

Take Action:

Speak truth gently: share one Scripture that steadies anxious thoughts (no commentary needed).

DAY 31 BLESSING OVER HER LIFE AND MINISTRY

"The Lord bless you and keep you; the Lord make his face to shine upon you and be gracious to you; the Lord lift up his countenance upon you and give you peace."

— NUMBERS 6:24–26 (ESV)

Devotional Thought:

After 30 days of lifting up the pastor's wife in prayer, the final day is a time to speak blessing over her life and ministry. She pours out so much for others; her family, the church, and those in need. Today is an opportunity to ask God to pour back into her.

God delights in blessing His children. He longs to fill her with peace, joy, and rest. His grace is sufficient for every challenge she faces. As she continues her journey in ministry, may she walk in the assurance that His favor rests upon her.

Pray today that God's blessing will cover every area of her life. Ask that His favor will go before her and that she will experience His goodness in abundance.

Prayer:

Father, I thank You for _____. Bless her abundantly. Pour out Your grace upon her. Let Your favor surround her like a shield. Bless her marriage, her family, and her ministry. Fill her home with laughter and love. Strengthen her faith and renew her spirit. Let her see the fruit of her labor and know that her work is not in vain. Shine Your face upon her and give her peace. Walk with her every step of the journey ahead. May she feel Your presence and love today and always. In Jesus' name, Amen.

Take Action:

End with blessing: pray Numbers 6:24–26 over her and tell her you did.

TAKE ACTION IDEAS

DAY 1 – REMIND HER WHO SHE IS IN CHRIST

(Write one sentence confirming her identity in Christ and give it to her.)

If you don't know what to say, try:

1. "I just want you to know, you are deeply valued, not because of what you do, but because of who you are in Christ."
2. "Your quiet faithfulness reflects Jesus more than you probably realize."
3. "I see a woman who belongs to God before she belongs to any role."
4. "You carry grace with you, it's evident."
5. "You are not invisible. God sees you, and so do I."
6. "Your identity isn't 'pastor's wife' first, it's daughter of the King."

7. "The way you love your family shows your rootedness in Christ."
8. "You don't have to earn appreciation. You're already cherished."
9. Text version: "Just a reminder today, you are deeply loved by God."
10. Card version: Write John 15:15 and underline "I have called you friends."

Simple actions instead of words:

- Leave a handwritten card on her car.
- Mail a short, thoughtful note.
- Send a voice memo praying Scripture over her.
- Slip a verse card into her Bible at church.

DAY 2 – ENCOURAGE HER CALLING

(Send a 2–3 line encouragement naming something you appreciate about her role.)

If you don't know what to say, try:

1. "I'm thankful God placed you here in this season."
2. "Your presence in this church matters more than you know."
3. "You don't have to be anyone else. You're exactly who we need."
4. "I see how you support and pray. It makes a difference."
5. "Your leadership may be quiet, but it is powerful."
6. "You don't need to compare yourself. God chose you."
7. "The way you love people here is a gift."
8. "I'm grateful you said yes to this calling."

9. "I see your steadiness. It brings peace."
10. "You are equipped for this, even on the hard days."

Simple actions instead of words:

- Comment something specific after church ("That conversation you had with __ was so kind.")
- Post a brief public appreciation (appropriate and honoring).
- Bring flowers with a note that says, "Thank you for saying yes to God."
- Offer practical help tied to her calling (childcare during an event, set-up help, etc.).

DAY 6 – HER FRIENDSHIPS

(Be a safe friend. Invite connection with no agenda.)

If you don't know what to say, try:

1. "I'd love to grab coffee sometime, no church business, just us."
2. "You don't have to be 'on' with me."
3. "How are *you* doing? Not as a pastor's wife, just as you?"
4. "I'm here if you need to talk. I won't fix it or repeat it."
5. "I value you as a friend, not a role."
6. "If you ever need a break from ministry talk, I'm your person."
7. "I appreciate who you are, not just what you do."
8. "Let's take a walk this week."
9. "No expectations. Just friendship."

Simple actions instead of words:

- Invite her on a walk instead of a formal lunch. Meet her at a park if she has littles.
- Drop off coffee and sit for 20 relaxed minutes.
- Text: "Thinking of you. No response needed."
- Include her in something ordinary (errands, baking, school pickup).
- Keep everything she shares confidential, always.

DAY 8 – HER PRAYER LIFE: (ENCOURAGE HER PERSONAL TIME WITH THE LORD.)

If you don't know what to say, try:

1. "How can I pray specifically for you this week?"
2. "I prayed for you this morning."
3. "Is there something on your heart I can lift up?"
4. "Would you like me to pray with you right now?"
5. "I'm covering you in prayer this month."
6. "God sees you, even when others don't."
7. "I'm asking the Lord to refresh your spirit."
8. "You don't have to carry this alone — let's pray."
9. "May the Lord meet you in a deep way this week."
10. "I'm grateful for how you intercede for others."

Simple actions instead of words:

- Send a short voice memo prayer.
- Text a Scripture with "Praying this over you today."
- Pray with her before or after church quietly.
- Keep a 30-day prayer list with her name on it.
- Fast one meal and pray specifically for her.

DAY 9 – PROTECTION FROM BURNOUT

(Encourage rest and healthy priorities.)

If you don't know what to say, try:

1. "It's okay to rest."
2. "You don't have to do everything."
3. "We'd rather have you healthy than exhausted."
4. "It's okay to say no."
5. "You're allowed to take a break."
6. "Your worth isn't tied to productivity."
7. "Let us carry this one."
8. "You don't have to respond tonight."
9. "Please protect your rest."
10. "We care about *you*, not just your service."

Simple actions instead of words:

- Offer to handle one ministry task.
- Volunteer for event setup/cleanup.
- Babysit so she can rest.
- Drop off a meal during busy seasons.
- Publicly support a boundary she sets.

DAY 17 – HER HEART FOR SERVING: (SHOW APPRECIATION FOR WHAT SHE QUIETLY DOES.)

If you don't know what to say, try:

1. "I see how much you serve. Thank you."
2. "That detail you handled mattered."

3. "You don't get enough credit for what you do."
4. "Your hospitality blesses so many."
5. "I notice your consistency."
6. "Your kindness sets the tone."
7. "You make people feel welcome."
8. "Your behind-the-scenes work doesn't go unnoticed."
9. "Thank you for loving this church."
10. "Your faithfulness is beautiful."

Simple actions instead of words:

- Send flowers with "Thank you for serving."
- Leave a small gift card with a gratitude note.
- Publicly thank her (appropriately and sincerely).
- Step up and serve alongside her.
- Write a handwritten thank-you card.

DAY 19 – HER FAMILY RELATIONSHIPS: (SUPPORT HER HOME, NOT JUST HER MINISTRY.)

If you don't know what to say, try:

1. "Your family matters deeply to us."
2. "We're praying for your kids by name."
3. "How can we support your family this week?"
4. "You're doing a beautiful job as a mom."
5. "Your marriage is a blessing to witness."
6. "Please take the night off. We've got this."
7. "Your home is a testimony."
8. "We want your family protected."
9. "We respect your family time."
10. "Your kids are a gift to this church."

Simple actions instead of words:

- Bring a family meal.
- Give the kids small encouragement notes.
- Offer childcare during church events.
- Respect their day off fully.
- Gift a date-night voucher.

DAY 29 – MODELING GRATITUDE: (EXPRESS SINCERE APPRECIATION.)

If you don't know what to say, try:

1. "Thank you for loving our church."
2. "We're grateful you're here."
3. "Your presence is a gift."
4. "We don't say it enough — thank you."
5. "I appreciate your steady spirit."
6. "This church is better because of you."
7. "Thank you for the sacrifices you make."
8. "You are valued here."
9. "We are praying blessing over you."
10. "We see you."

Simple actions instead of words:

- Write a short public appreciation post (with honor and discretion).
- Organize a small appreciation basket.
- Have the church sign a simple thank-you card.
- Send a handwritten note in the mail.
- Tell her in person, sincerely and briefly.

SIMPLE WAYS TO STRENGTHEN HER THIS YEAR

- Send a handwritten note twice a year.
- Drop off a meal during a heavy church season.
- Text a Scripture after Sunday.
- Offer childcare without fanfare.
- Invite her to coffee with no agenda.
- Defend her gently in conversations.
- Celebrate small wins publicly.
- Respect her boundaries.
- Ask how you can pray and actually follow up.
- Remember her children by name.

PRAYER PROMPTS FOR WHEN YOU DON'T KNOW WHAT TO SAY

Pray for Her:

- Identity in Christ
- Rest
- Protection from comparison
- Emotional resilience
- Deep friendships

Pray for Her Marriage:

- Unity
- Protection
- Joy
- Private strength

Pray for Her Children:

- Security
- Faith
- Protection from resentment

STARTING A PRAYER TEAM FOR YOUR CHURCH LEADERS

A single month of prayer is powerful.

A sustained culture of prayer is transformative.

Many churches find that after completing these 31 days, they do not want the covering to stop. What began as individual intercession becomes a shared conviction: our leaders and their families need steady support.

Scripture reminds us that *"The prayer of a righteous person has great power as it is working."* — James 5:16

Fervent, faithful prayer is not symbolic. It accomplishes real spiritual work.

A small, consistent prayer team can quietly strengthen:

- The spiritual resilience of your pastor
- The emotional health of his wife
- The unity of their marriage
- The security of their children
- The long-term stability of your church

You may never see all that your prayers hold together, but its weight is eternal.

HOW TO BEGIN

A leader prayer team does not need to be large. It needs to be faithful.

Start simply:

1. Identify 3–5 mature, discreet women.

Choose those who understand confidentiality and spiritual responsibility.

2. Establish clear guardrails.

This is not a discussion group. It is a prayer covering.

3. Meet monthly or quarterly.

Consistency matters more than frequency.

4. Pray Scripture, not speculation.

Let God's Word shape your requests.

5. Protect trust.

Confidentiality is essential. What is shared in prayer remains there.

THE BENEFITS OF A DEDICATED PRAYER TEAM

When a church commits to praying intentionally for its leaders, it often sees:

- Reduced burnout
- Stronger marriages
- Greater congregational unity
- Deeper trust between leadership and church members
- A culture of honor rather than criticism

Prayer shifts the tone of a church.

It cultivates generosity instead of expectation.

It builds protection instead of pressure.

It strengthens the woman who so often strengthens everyone else.

If your church would like guidance in establishing or strengthening a leader prayer culture — or in building secure, sustainable support around your pastor's wife and family — we would be honored to serve you.

For implementation support, prayer team development, or church-wide Prayer Pledge initiatives, please contact:

info@cedarcreekministries.org

A healthy church is built not only on strong preaching, but on faithful intercession.

And the quiet strength behind a pastor matters more than most will ever know.

RECOGNIZING WHEN SHE MAY NEED EXTRA COVERING

Pastor's wives are often strong, capable, and deeply committed to their calling. They may not easily voice when they are weary.

This is not a call to monitor her.

It is a call to be attentive in prayer.

There may be seasons when she needs additional spiritual covering. You may notice:

- Withdrawal from community or reduced visibility
- Constant availability without visible rest
- Chronic exhaustion or over-functioning
- Guarded communication
- A quiet loss of joy
- Increased isolation
- Tension around her family life

These signs are not accusations. They are invitations to intercede.

You do not need to know details to pray effectively.

Ask the Lord to:

- Restore her joy
- Strengthen her body
- Protect her marriage
- Guard her children
- Renew her calling
- Surround her with wise and trustworthy friends

Prayer is not only for crisis.

It is for prevention.

It is for protection.

It is for steady reinforcement before cracks appear.

A church that prays before burnout builds resilience that lasts.

A FINAL BLESSING

As you close this journal, may you remember that prayer is never small.

May the Lord make you a faithful intercessor; steady, humble, and strong.

May your prayers rise like a quiet shield around the woman who stands beside your pastor.

May God guard her heart, strengthen her body, protect her marriage, and give her deep, enduring joy.

May her home be marked by peace.

May her friendships be life-giving.

May her calling remain secure in Christ.

And may your church grow in honor, generosity, and spiritual maturity as you choose to carry one another's burdens.

The work of intercession is often unseen.

But heaven sees.

And God is faithful to sustain what His people cover in prayer.

ABOUT CEDAR CREEK MINISTRIES

Cedar Creek Ministries exists to strengthen church leaders and the families who stand beside them.

We believe healthy churches are built on more than vision and programming. They are sustained by faithful prayer, secure leadership homes, and a culture of honor that protects those who carry spiritual responsibility.

Over the years, we have had the privilege of walking alongside pastors and their wives in a variety of seasons; times of growth, times of transition, and times of quiet endurance. Through these relationships, one truth has remained clear:

When leaders are supported well, churches flourish.

Our heart is simple:

- To cultivate prayer cultures that protect leadership families
- To equip churches with practical tools for sustainable ministry
- To strengthen the woman behind the pastor without placing additional pressure on her
- To help churches move from appreciation to intentional support

Cedar Creek Ministries provides:

- Prayer resources for churches and leadership teams
- Prayer Pledge Drive tools and implementation guidance
- Leader prayer team development
- Support frameworks for strengthening pastoral families

We are committed to building trust, honoring confidentiality, and serving churches with integrity and humility.

If your church would like guidance in developing a sustainable prayer culture for your leaders, we would be honored to come alongside you.

For more information or to connect with our team:

info@cedarcreekministries.org

A strong church begins with strong leadership.

Strong leadership is sustained by faithful intercession.

CONTINUE STEADFASTLY

Let your prayers continue long after these pages are filled.

The quiet strength of a church is often found

in the unseen faithfulness of its people.

Stand steady.

Pray faithfully.

Honor generously.

Made in the USA
Coppell, TX
27 February 2026

72448834R00066